Collaborating
in the Workplace

A Guide for Building Better Teams

By Ike Lasater

With Julie Stiles

PuddleDancer
PRESS

2240 Encinitas Blvd., Ste. D-911, Encinitas, CA 92024
email@PuddleDancer.com • www.PuddleDancer.com

For additional information:
Center for Nonviolent Communication
9301 Indian School Rd., NE, Suite 204, Albuquerque, NM 87112
Ph: 505-244-4041 • Fax: 505-247-0414 • Email: cnvc@cnvc.org • Website: www.cnvc.org

Collaborating in the Workplace
A Guide for Building Better Teams

© 2019 PuddleDancer Press
A PuddleDancer Press Book

PuddleDancer Press, Permissions Dept.
2240 Encinitas Blvd., Ste. D-911, Encinitas, CA 92024
Tel: 760-652-5754 Fax: 760-274-6400
www.NonviolentCommunication.com Email@PuddleDancer.com

Ordering Information
Please contact Independent Publishers Group, Tel: 312-337-0747;
Fax: 312-337-5985; Email: frontdesk@ipgbook.com or visit www.IPGbook.com
for other contact information and details about ordering online

Author: Ike Lasater
Editor: Julie Stiles
Cover and Interior Design: Shannon Bodie, Lightbourne.com
Cover source photo: www.istock.com, Peopleimages

Manufactured in the United States of America,
1st Printing, April 2019
♻ Printed on recycled paper

23 22 21 20 19   1 2 3 4 5

ISBN: 978-1-934336-16-8

Library of Congress Cataloging-in-Publication Data

Names: Lasater, Ike, author. | Stiles, Julie, author.
Title: Collaborating in the workplace : a guide for building better teams /
    Ike Lasater ; with Julie Stiles.
Description: Encinitas, CA : PuddleDancer Press, [2019] | Includes bibliographical
    references and index.
Identifiers: LCCN 2018035906| ISBN 9781934336168 (trade paper : alk. paper) |
    ISBN 9781934336229 (ePUB) | ISBN 9781934336281 (ebook pdf) |
    ISBN 9781934336342 (mobi/kindle)
Subjects: LCSH: Teams in the workplace. | Violence in the workplace--Prevention. |
    Communication in personnel management.
Classification: LCC HD66 .L373 2019 | DDC 658.4/022--dc23
LC record available at https://lccn.loc.gov/2018035906

Endorsements of
Collaborating in the Workplace

"I have used the exercises in this book with the participants of my Leadership Development Training and have witnessed the dramatic impact empathy has in a successful collaborative balancing act. I highly recommend *Collaborating in the Workplace* as a tool to improve both your team's management and its relationships. This book has the power to develop the vision and the skills necessary to achieve team cohesion and the dream of unity to which more and more organizations aspire."

—GIOVANNA CASTOLDI, Nonviolent Communication
Certified Trainer, Founder of "School of Feedback"

"Recently, the business press has been telling us to build empathy and 'emotional intelligence' into our organizations' cultures, promising us more effectiveness through empowerment, trust, and mutuality. Sounds great in a workshop, but . . . conflict often is a daily reality in business, and people soon fall back into their old patterns. Finally, here's a book that provides a clear and actionable approach that you can start using right away. Ike Lasater has a lifetime's experience helping organizations and individuals learn how to navigate conflicts. Ike presents specific techniques and practices to help team members become more open to one another's creativity, so that—together—they can harness the energy that conflict often dissipates. Use the wisdom of this book to make your culture more resilient, your team more effective, and your work more satisfying."

—ED NIEHAUS, Chairman,
Collaborative Drug Discovery, Inc.

"Business people understand the importance of effective teams, but often aren't clear about how to develop the actual skills of collaboration. Ike Lasater provides this clarity. His many years of teaching the art of connection have resulted in this groundbreaking book. Once a team learns to communicate by connecting with self and others, they will never want to go back to functioning at a lower level. Every company would be wise to permanently place this book in the middle of their conference table and refer to it daily!"

—RITA MARIE JOHNSON, CEO, Rasur Foundation
International Creator of the Connection Practice,
Author, *Completely Connected: Uniting Our
Empathy & Insight for Extraordinary Results*

"Ike and I have been close colleagues and collaborators for over fifteen years, and this book is a powerful distillation and integration of the work for organizations. Ike and Julie lay out in clear, practical, and doable ways the core, and I believe universal, skills and maps for navigating interpersonal conflict and developing highly effective teamwork. *Collaborating in the Workplace: A Guide for Building Better Teams* provides skills and practices that will make any organization more successful and employees more fulfilled. This work will be common practice in organizations of the future."

—JOHN KINYON, CNVC trainer and cofounder of
Mediate Your Life training, coaching, and mediation,
Author, *From Conflict to Connection: Transforming
Difficult Conversations Into Peaceful Resolutions*,
www.mediateyourlife.com

Contents

Acknowledgments

I could never have gotten these ideas to print without Julie Stiles. She and I have been working together as a writing team since 2005. I also want to thank all of the participants in my workshops, where I work out these ideas.

American psychologist Marshall Rosenberg, PhD, developed much of what underlies the approach in this manual, particularly the terminology and processes related to needs and requests, as part of a communication process he named "Nonviolent Communication" or "NVC."

Rosenberg distinguished among four components of communication, all of which will be referenced and explored within the following pages:

- **Observations** (versus judgments)
- **Feelings** (versus "faux" feelings)
- **Needs** (versus strategies)
- **Requests** (versus demands)

He made suggestions as to how to think of these components in our communication in order to create connection with ourselves and with others. He developed the following terms:

- **Self-Empathy**: When communicating with yourself
- **Self-Expression**: To communicate what is going on with you out loud to others
- **Silent Empathy**: When you are silently guessing within yourself what is going on within another person
- **Empathy**: When you are guessing out loud what is going on within another person

I particularly appreciate Rosenberg's insights regarding requests.

I also want to acknowledge and appreciate John Kinyon for the years of insight and learning that resulted from our long collaboration—which first began in 2002—as cofounders of Mediate Your Life.

—Ike Lasater

Introduction

What Makes an Effective Team?

Teams are where business is done. Whether it's a team within one department, an interdisciplinary or interdepartmental group, or a team that includes outside parties such as contractors or clients, it's people working together that creates success.

Yet, not all teams are effective. Some groups seem to gel and work together effortlessly, whereas in others strife and struggle seem to be the norm, with work progressing in fits and starts. Why the difference? What makes an effective team, and more important, how can your employees learn to create teams that crystallize instead of clash?

Let's start examining these questions with a brief discussion of what an effective team is and the research on what makes good ones work. I'll then identify a set of skills that, when adopted, lead to the characteristics of effective teamwork.

Effective Teams

What is meant by "effective" teamwork? While definitions may differ, when I talk about it I'm referring to a group of people who work well together to create outstanding outcomes. After all, this is in the realm of business, where results matter. While many approaches focus on how to set objectives and reach them, interpersonal skills are important to ensure that the team collaborates well to achieve their outcomes.

Interpersonal skills are often referred to in business as "soft skills." Though this term implies a devaluing of these skills, in fact more and more employers and leaders recognize that soft skills are important. As many as three-quarters of business leaders think that these skills are even more important than job-specific (so called "hard") skills.[1] Yet there's also a skills gap here, as many people and businesses focus their skill-building and professional development offerings on the job-specific skills, not on communication and collaboration.

Most people began learning their social interaction skills in preschool—we were (hopefully) taught how to play well in the sandbox. There's a prevailing assumption that if you learned those skills in preschool, you will continue to play well with others now. Yet, as any manager knows, often the interpersonal skills that allow a team to be effective are missing.

Fortunately, there's an increasingly large body of research pointing toward what makes an effective team and the skills that matter most. As one example, Patrick Lencioni has written extensively about teams, both what makes them work and what doesn't. He identifies five dysfunctions of a team: absence of trust, fear of conflict, lack of commitment, avoidance of accountability, and inattention to results. He suggests that some of the characteristics of a high performing team include comfort in asking for help and admitting mistakes and taking risks in offering feedback.[2]

Recent research at Google points in a similar direction, showing that what distinguishes effective teams is *how people interact*. Having the right set of behavioral norms makes teams better at working together and achieving their goals, because these norms create a sense of psychological safety. People feel like they can take interpersonal risks and speak their mind without fear of embarrassment or rejection. Respect and trust characterize the interactions between team members. What are the norms that researchers identified? First, people share the stage approximately equally, so everyone on the team contributes, raising the collective intelligence. Second, people exhibit social sensitivity—they intuit how others are feeling based on nonverbal cues. In other words, they empathize.[3]

Thus, with an increasing amount of work being done in teams or through collaboration,[4] it pays to pay attention to the skills that make effective collaboration possible.

The Skills That Matter

So what are some of the skills that are essential for teams to work? Here are some of the skills I've found that increase team effectiveness.

Self-Connection

Connecting with yourself is a fundamental skill that helps you return to presence and choice when experiencing a stress response. Interactions at work often trigger a basic Fight-Flight-Freeze response—people interpret some level of danger. Experiencing stress limits our options to respond in a way that enhances collaboration, whereas connecting to ourselves gives us a greater possibility to connect with others. While lots of means of self-connection exist, I use a simple breath-body-needs practice that can be done as a daily exercise and quickly in the heat of the moment.

Listening

One of the fundamental skills that helps build *psychological safety* among people is to listen. Most people may think they listen fairly well already, but I'm talking about listening to the speaker's satisfaction (not to the listener's). That means including a few other skills that help the speaker know that they've been heard, such as listening for the needs they're trying to meet, repeating back what the listener heard and checking if that was what the speaker wanted to be heard, and clarifying what the speaker would like from the interaction. It's listening that includes empathy.

Why is listening in this way so important? Because when people know they've been heard to their satisfaction, and then in turn they hear others in the same way, it *builds trust* between people. With this kind of listening, over time people know they can be vulnerable. They can say the things that might be difficult to say, yet would help the team move forward, with the confidence that there will not be personal repercussions.

Making Clear Requests and Agreements

The ability to make clear requests and agreements (and help others make them too) is another fundamental skill that is unfortunately not taught, as it is essential to teamwork. In teams where these skills are lacking, requests may be vague and open to interpretation. People may leave a meeting without a well-defined understanding of who is doing what and by when. These skills ensure that everyone is on the same page, and support people to be more *accountable* and pay more attention to *results*.

Having Difficult Conversations

Any time two or more people work together, conflict is likely to occur. In fact, in team situations, conflict between different perspectives is often necessary to arrive at solutions that will create greater success. Yet these are often missed opportunities, due to the fear of conflict and the inability to have these potentially difficult conversations in a way that creates connection and resolves the conflict with forward movement.

In truth, there are multiple skills at work here. One is the ability to prepare for a conversation through addressing any judgments of the other people, the situation, or yourself. Another is the ability to have the conversation with a level of presence that allows people to listen to one another even when tensions rise. Finally, there's a skill to debriefing the conversation so that instead of going into more judgment, people learn from what occurred and are then better able to meet their needs going forward.

Taking these skills together, there's a clear cycle here that I call the learning cycle. When team members can prepare, have, and debrief their conversation, interactions can take on an upward spiraling effect, with people using the self-reflective process to continuously work toward their own and the team's needs. As these conversations become the group norm, the elements of *psychological safety* are generated in this repeated cycle. Respectful conversations where people listen in order to create connection engender *trust*. People also develop increased *social sensitivity* as they are more attuned to listening for what's going on behind someone's words.

As the team creates, one conversation at a time, their creations are then enhanced as the team works ever better together.

Interrupting

People are often taught it's impolite to interrupt. In my view, it's actually more impolite to let a person continue beyond what I can take in. Since people are taught not to interrupt, however, they're also not taught the skill of interrupting in a way that creates connection instead of disconnection.

In a team meeting, knowing how to interrupt is a valuable skill, as it can help keep people on track, get to the point more quickly, and foster cohesiveness. This is not interrupting for interruptions sake or to get your point across—it's interrupting to increase clarity, make a request, or create something greater for the group as a whole.

Giving and Receiving Feedback

Feedback is crucial to team members' ability to learn and grow as well as to the team being able to work together successfully. Most people have experienced attempts to give feedback that backfired—whether on the giving or receiving end. In my view, this is often because people are disconnected, either from themselves or from one another.

Learning the skill of giving feedback while focusing on the quality of connection makes it more likely the feedback will contribute to the receiver. When this skill is present, people can also receive feedback—even that given judgmentally—in a positive and enriching manner. Finally, knowing how to give feedback from connection increases the likelihood that people will take risks in offering it—one of the characteristics of a high performing team.

Expressing Appreciation

Expressing appreciation or gratitude is actually a subset of giving feedback, however it's helpful to separate it as a separate skill since, in some places, expressing appreciation is such an alien concept. The way it was expressed in my boyhood and the people I worked with was, "Why would I say 'good job'—they're supposed to do a good job! I'll tell them when they *aren't* doing a good job!" Unfortunately, this is all too often the prevailing attitude in the workplace.

Nonetheless, especially in teamwork, expressing appreciation goes a long way toward creating a culture not only where people work well together, but also where outcomes shine. People who feel valued and acknowledged are often desirous of contributing even more. Building into a team the norms of expressing gratitude, acknowledging others for their contribution, and celebrating when things go well engender increased respect and trust. These are exactly the kind of overlooked soft skills that produce excellent teams.

Why Focus on Interpersonal Skills?

One of the difficulties for business leaders is that often it's only when obvious dysfunction exists that the need for these kinds of communication skills surfaces. In reality, I would argue that these skills are essential to a business thriving and ultimately reaching its goals. But, how do we describe and justify the benefits of spending time and money on developing these skills in the workforce?

It's easier to talk about the benefit of team members learning these skills through what is avoided. When people have the skills I've listed above, it reduces the likelihood of misinterpretations, and when those do happen, people have the skills to work them out without hurt feelings. Negative and destructive conflicts are avoided, as is the tendency for "under-the-surface" conflict that isn't addressed to undermine relationships and the team.

When people are in touch with themselves and what needs they would like met, they are less likely to say things that create disruption, and more likely to say things that create connection. If people aren't connected to themselves, it's difficult (if not impossible) to be connected to others, and without connection, it's difficult (if not impossible) to effectively collaborate.

The skills help people be more present as well as connected to themselves, which has myriad benefits, including being clearer about their goals and priorities. Being part of a team means that professional goals are tied to team goals. One person who has clarity about goals helps the entire team hone in on the team's goals and the appropriate steps to achieve them. In addition, being present with yourself increases your enjoyment and satisfaction, helps reduce stress, and creates resilience. If you enjoy your life more, you tend to play in the sandbox well and produce a better product.

Encouraging a self-reflective process within a team enhances all of the aspects that support effective teams and boosts the sense of psychological safety that is so important to teamwork. When your employees are collaborating well, their collective intelligence is greater than the sum of its parts, generating higher quality decisions and wasting less time and resources. Collaboration—and the skills that foster it—allow for the kind of creativity and innovation that characterizes the most successful companies.

How to Use This Book

I've worked in the field of communication, conflict resolution, and mediation for more than twenty years. During that time, I've trained and coached people in more than twenty countries worldwide and countless cultures. I've yet to find a culture in which the approach that is outlined in this book does not work. Why? Because it's fundamentally based on what is true for all of us as human beings, which runs deeper than cultural, linguistic, and national overlays. When we can meet one another as human beings first, we can find a way to collaborate.

I wrote this book to help you and your team members learn the skills that foster successful collaboration, and it draws heavily from Nonviolent Communication (NVC), a way of thinking and speaking that is particularly effective in reducing stress and conflict, creating connection, and improving collaboration.

To begin, you'll learn the foundations in Part I. The Fight-Flight-Freeze stress response, which commonly shows up in conflict situations, is our starting point, which will help you begin to recognize your triggers. I then introduce a vocabulary for naming feelings and needs—key components to this model of communication. You'll subsequently learn to apply these components in the Self-Connection Process, which is your foundation to help you return to presence and choice in situations when you are experiencing the stress response.

In Part II, you will then go on to apply these foundations in conversation. You'll practice communication skills to listen to others and be listened to, make powerful requests, prepare for and practice difficult conversations, and debrief for resilience.

Part III will cover additional applications of these skills for team collaboration, including how to interrupt effectively, give and receive meaningful and productive feedback, and express appreciation. You will practice using the inevitable challenges within the team as opportunities to connect, both with yourself and your colleagues, thus improving productivity and reducing interpersonal conflict and stress.

All of these skills make it more likely that your teams will thrive in an environment that encourages individual risk taking, and where members listen to one another's ideas regardless of the perceived differences in power within the team.

While these are the foundational skills for effective communication and collaboration, this book is not (and is not intended to be) a definitive guide to all aspects of working in teams. For a team to be effective, other pieces must be in place, such as goals, deadlines, and metrics to measure success. Other works cover these essential aspects of team collaboration, so I do not cover them here. Nonetheless, you'll notice that the creation and maintenance of all other aspects of teamwork require and rely on effective communication. Thus, this book provides the bedrock that will help all other teamwork components to be on firm ground.

While reading this book is helpful, the only way it can make a difference in your team is through practice. Each section includes step-by-step instructions to guide you through learning the skills, and most of them are best learned by practicing with others. To help you with this, included is a section on setting up a successful practice structure, using the flight simulator metaphor. Whether you practice with people on your team or not is up to you. While the ideal situation is for all team members to be learning and practicing these skills together, you can still make a difference even if you're the only person on your team utilizing them. If you'd like to become more knowledgeable and proficient using these kinds of skills internally as well, make sure to check out the earlier companion to this work, *Words That Work in Business*.

The innovative team of the future is one where the skills of collaboration are vital to success. This book offers the building blocks upon which collaboration will grow.

1. Infographic: Communicating in the Modern Workplace. http://online.queens.edu/onlineprograms/mba/resources/infographic/communicating-in-the-workplace

2. Patrick Lencioni, *The Five Dysfunctions of a Team: A Leadership Fable* (San Francisco: Jossey-Bass, 2002).

3. Charles Duhigg, "What Google Learned From Its Quest to Build The Perfect Team," *New York Times*, February 25, 2016. https://www.nytimes.com/2016/02/28/magazine/what-google-learned-from-its-quest-to-build-the-perfect-team.html?smid=pl-share

4. Rob Cross, Reb Rebele and Adam Grant, "Collaborative Overload," *Harvard Business Review*, January–February 2016. https://hbr.org/2016/01/collaborative-overload

Part I

Foundations

What happens for you when you are in a difficult conversation? How aware are you of your triggers, and what happens physiologically for you when you are stressed? What can you do to stay present when this occurs?

Most people are not trained to be able to respond well when triggered. They get angry, go into their habitual reaction pattern, and then berate themselves (and/or others) afterward and vow to change and be more in control the next time. Then another trigger arises, and the pattern repeats.

In this section, you'll learn how to break that pattern. Recognizing when you are in a stress response and how you normally react, you'll be able to apply two key components of your experience—feelings and needs—using the Self-Connection Process to reconnect to yourself and be able to act in a way that more accurately reflects your values. In other words, instead of reacting, you will be present enough to act—to choose how you respond.

This simple (yet not always easy) skill is a first step to being able to be in disagreement and difficult conversations with teammates and coworkers without being in conflict. Let's get started.

Fight-Flight-Freeze (The Stress Response)

All too often in modern day-to-day interactions, people react to what is happening around them as though their physical well-being is being challenged. The human body only has one way to respond to perceived challenge, regardless of whether it is an actual physical threat or simply an unwelcome comment at the water cooler. The way the body reacts to both is by releasing stress hormones such as adrenaline, norepinephrine, and cortisol into our bloodstream.

This process is referred to as the Fight-Flight-Freeze response, or alternatively, as the Stress Response.

The Stress Response serves you when you need to protect yourself from physical danger, like when a lion on the savanna is attacking you. Nonetheless, in work and home environments, triggering the Stress Response because you are dreading an upcoming conversation or because you are upset by an interaction with a colleague not only serves to reduce your effectiveness, but also is harmful to your health.

Once the deeper parts of the brain are triggered into the fight-flight-freeze survival reaction, it's difficult to think clearly and sequentially, and the conscious mind tends to be flooded with thoughts about who is right, who is wrong, and who deserves punishment. In addition, people will tend to respond to similar situations according to habitual patterns of thoughts and actions that they have developed over the course of their life, and it becomes very difficult to apply the language and communication skills they possess.

As a consequence of the release of these stress hormones, peripheral vision narrows, and blood is shunted to the muscles for flight or to fight and away from reproduction and immune function. The hands moisten and you are likely to feel shaky.

If you do not do something to stop the release of stress hormones, it's less likely you will be able to think clearly, sequentially, and logically, and you will tend to act in ways that are contrary to your values.

Finally, as you come down from the Stress Response, you may experience an adrenaline hangover, the symptoms of which are lack of motivation, fatigue and weakness, thirst, headaches and muscle aches, nausea, vomiting or stomach pain, poor or decreased sleep, increased sensitivity to light and sound, dizziness or a sense of the room spinning, and shakiness.

EXERCISE

Think through a recent interaction with someone that was difficult for you. What was your experience? Consider each of the following and see if you can identify how the stress response shows up in your mind, body, and behavior:

1. What sensations did you experience? (Where were you tense or holding, how was your heart rate and breathing, what changes in temperature did you experience, what other sensations and feelings were present?)

2. What was happening in your mind? (What were you perceiving about the situation, what beliefs or judgments did you hold about yourself or the other person, what thoughts were present?)

3. What was your behavior? (Did you go into fight, flight, or freeze? What did you actually say or do, and how was that behavior similar to or different from how you normally respond in similar situations?)

Being able to recognize when you're in the stress response is the first step to being able to change it. Next, we will look at two building blocks that will support you in reconnecting to yourself when you're triggered—needs and feelings.

Universal Human Needs

The term *needs*, as used here, refers to the motives for conduct. For instance, all humans need water, air, touch, connection with others, fun, play, meaning, care, intimacy, etc. Everyone wants these needs met in order to survive, and more than that, to have satisfying and meaningful lives.

All too often, people become fixated on a *particular way* of meeting a need—a specific *strategy*. This fixation can become the source of conflict within oneself and with others. Yet a need is never tied to one single strategy—there are always multiple ways to meet a need. Knowing what you need (and what others need) from moment to moment helps you find strategies that will meet your needs and theirs. And, knowing the needs you are seeking to meet with a particular strategy can help expand the possibilities that might meet those needs.

When people are not aware of their own needs, they tend to spend more of their time reacting to one another, and this often creates havoc in their lives. The core needs (on pages 15 and 16) are grouped into three main categories and nine subcategories.

EXERCISE

Using the list of needs below, see if you can identify your needs in each of the following:

1. You are reading this book right now, what need are you seeking to meet in reading it?
2. Think of one action you took earlier today. What need were you acting from?
3. What needs are you meeting with the work that you do? What additional needs would you like to be met in your job or career?
4. Consider the situation you used in looking at your stress response. What needs of yours were not met in that situation?

WELL-BEING

Sustenance/Health	Safety/Security	Beauty/Peace/Play
abundance/thriving	comfort	acceptance
exercise	confidence	appreciation
food/nutrition	emotional safety	gratitude
nourishment	familiarity	awareness
rest/sleep	order	balance
relaxation	structure	ease
shelter	predictability	equanimity
sustainability	protection from	humor
support/help	harm	presence
wellness	stability	rejuvenation
vitality	trust	simplicity
energy	faith	space
		tranquillity
		wholeness
		wonder

CONNECTION

Love/Caring	Empathy/Understanding	Community/Belonging
affection/warmth	awareness/clarity	cooperation
beauty	acceptance	fellowship
closeness/touch	acknowledgment	generosity
companionship	communication	inclusion
compassion	consideration	interdependence
kindness	hearing (hear/be heard)	harmony/peace
intimacy	knowing (know/be known)	hospitality/welcoming
mattering	presence/listening	mutuality
importance	respect/equality	reciprocity
nurturing	receptivity/openness	partnership
sexual connection	recognition	relationship
respect	seeing (see/be seen)	support/solidarity
honoring	self-esteem	trust/dependability
valuing/prizing	sensitivity	transparency/openness

SELF-EXPRESSION

Autonomy/ Freedom	Authenticity	Meaning/ Contribution
choice	adventure	appreciation/
clarity	aliveness	gratitude
congruence	discovery	achievement
consistency	honesty	productivity
continuity	initiative	celebration/
dignity	innovation	mourning
freedom	inspiration	challenge
independence	joy	efficacy
integrity	mystery	effectiveness
power	passion	excellence
empowerment	spontaneity	growth
self-responsibility		learning/clarity
		mystery
		participation
		purpose/value
		self-actualization
		self-esteem
		skill/mastery

Feelings

Feelings are bodily sensations that signal whether your needs are being met by what is going on around you as well as inside you. Positive feelings tend to indicate needs met, and negative ones, needs not met.

Paying attention to your feelings when asked (by yourself or someone else) about a particular need, you are able to identify which needs the nonverbal parts of yourself interpret as met or not met. With practice, you will learn the signals from your body that tell you if the need you have guessed or your practice partner has guessed is accurate at that moment in time.

Feelings give you important additional information with which to navigate your internal and external worlds. When you have this additional information, you do not have to react to your feeling states out of habitual patterns of action, the early versions of which were learned in childhood and typically have been built upon and reinforced. Instead, you can examine your life with an eye to how you can better meet your needs and the needs of others.

For example, if you feel angry, instead of reacting as you normally would, you can inquire into what needs aren't met and then choose to try something different than your patterns would dictate. Choosing responses that are different than your habitual patterns allows you to learn how to free yourself from the mindlessness of these habits. This process of personal learning gives you insight not only into yourself, but also into the interior lives of others. So, feelings can be seen as a doorway to learning deeply about yourself and others.

The feelings on the next page are a selection of the hundreds of feeling words that exist in the English language.

EXERCISE

Using the list of feelings on the next page, see if you can identify your feelings in each of the following:

1. Think of a recent time when you had fun. What feeling arises in you now recalling that time?
2. Think of a meeting you attended recently at work. What feeling arises in you now recalling that meeting?
3. Think of where you are and where you'd like to be in your career. What feelings come up as you consider those?
4. Think of the situation you used in looking at your stress response. What feeling arises in you now recalling that situation?

PEACEFUL	LOVING	GLAD	PLAYFUL	INTERESTED
tranquil	warm	happy	energetic	involved
calm	affectionate	excited	effervescent	inquisitive
content	tender	hopeful	invigorated	intense
engrossed	appreciative	joyful	zestful	enriched
absorbed	friendly	satisfied	refreshed	absorbed
expansive	sensitive	delighted	impish	alert
serene	compassionate	encouraged	alive	aroused
loving	grateful	grateful	lively	astonished
blissful	nurtured	confident	exuberant	concerned
satisfied	amorous	inspired	giddy	curious
relaxed	trusting	touched	adventurous	eager
relieved	open	proud	mischievous	enthusiastic
quiet	thankful	exhilarated	jubilant	fascinated
carefree	radiant	ecstatic	goofy	intrigued
composed	adoring	optimistic	buoyant	surprised
fulfilled	passionate	glorious	electrified	helpful

MAD	SAD	SCARED	TIRED	CONFUSED
impatient	lonely	afraid	exhausted	frustrated
pessimistic	heavy	fearful	fatigued	perplexed
disgruntled	troubled	terrified	inert	hesitant
frustrated	helpless	startled	lethargic	troubled
irritable	gloomy	nervous	indifferent	uncomfortable
edgy	overwhelmed	jittery	weary	withdrawn
grouchy	distant	horrified	overwhelmed	apathetic
agitated	despondent	anxious	fidgety	embarrassed
exasperated	discouraged	worried	helpless	hurt
disgusted	distressed	anguished	heavy	uneasy
irked	dismayed	lonely	sleepy	irritated
cantankerous	disheartened	insecure	disinterested	suspicious
animosity	despairing	sensitive	reluctant	unsteady
bitter	sorrowful	shocked	passive	puzzled
rancorous	unhappy	apprehensive	dull	restless
irate, furious	depressed	dread	bored	boggled
angry	blue	jealous	listless	chagrined
hostile	miserable	desperate	blah	unglued
enraged	dejected	suspicious	mopey	detached
violent	melancholy	frightened	comatose	skeptical

Faux Feelings

Since most people were not taught much about feelings, it's important when considering them to distinguish between what is actually a feeling and words that people tend to treat like feelings but aren't. These "faux feelings" are words that actually imply that someone is doing something to you and generally connote wrongness or blame.

Below are just a few examples of faux feelings (see the Appendix for a more complete list) and examples of what a person might be really feeling when they use this particular faux feeling word. Notice that there are multiple feelings listed—this is a key way to tell if a word is a faux feeling. For example, if someone says, "I feel abandoned" they could conceivably be frightened, angry, or lonely. Using a faux feeling word doesn't actually give the information of how the person is feeling. The list below also includes unmet needs that might be motivating the use of the faux feeling word.

EXERCISE

Read through the list of faux feelings below and on the next page, along with the feelings and needs. Which ones have you used before? Start to notice in your thoughts and conversation when you are using faux feelings, and internally translate those into your feelings and needs.

FAUX FEELING	FEELING(S)	NEED(S)
Attacked	Scared, angry	Safety
Betrayed	Angry, hurt, disappointed, enraged	Trust, dependability, honesty, honor
Bullied	Angry, scared, pressured	Autonomy, choice, safety, consideration
Criticized	In pain, scared, anxious, humiliated	Understanding, acknowledgment, recognition

FAUX FEELING	FEELING(S)	NEED(S)
Insulted	Angry, embarrassed	Respect, consideration, peace
Manipulated	Angry, scared, powerless, thwarted, frustrated	Autonomy, empowerment, trust, equality, freedom, free choice, connection, genuineness
Pressured	Anxious, resentful, overwhelmed	Relaxation, clarity, space, consideration
Taken for granted	Sad, angry, hurt, disappointed	Appreciation, acknowledgment, recognition, consideration
Unappreciated	Sad, angry, hurt, frustrated	Appreciation, respect, acknowledgment
Wronged	Angry, hurt, resentful, irritated	Respect, justice, trust, safety, fairness

These are selections from a list developed in April 2000 for the Wisconsin International Intensive Training, an NVC workshop, edited by Susan Skye.

Now that you're familiar with your stress response, feelings, and needs, let's put it all together with a process that can help you reconnect in times you most would like to act from presence instead of react from habit: the Self-Connection Process.

The Self-Connection Process

When people perceive a challenge to their well-being, they're triggered into the stress response and typically are not able to act in ways that are consistent with their values, often later regretting their actions.

During the stress response, you can do specific things to become conscious of the needs you want to meet and how you want to meet them. As you become aware of how the stress response feels in your body, you will be able to use the Self-Connection Process to respond more effectively in these moments of stress. Thus, this process is a way to return to presence and choice in times of stress so that you have access to and can act according to your values.

It's imperative to practice how you want to act when experiencing the stress response. The ancient Greeks knew this more than 2600 years ago:

In adversity, we do not rise to the level of our expectations. We fall to the level of our training.

—Archilochus, Greek soldier and poet, c. 650 BC

Training is thus essential to be able to act as you would like to when you are under stress. That is why first responders, military, medical personnel, and others have increasingly trained in simulated real situations. They want to be feeling the rush of the stress response when they are training. They want the pretend situation to "feel" like the real situation, so they can practice how to respond in the heat of the moment.

Both science and the wisdom traditions point to the benefits of focusing on your breathing and bodily experience in order to reconnect and return to presence. With regular practice of the Self-Connection Process, you will build the capacity to respond more effectively in the midst of situations you perceive as emotionally or physically challenging. In addition, daily practice of the Self-Connection Process will remind you of your needs and the benefit of seeking to better meet needs over focusing on avoiding punishment.

You are encouraged to set aside at least five minutes a day to practice the Self-Connection Process, and also to practice throughout the day in as many moments as you can. The more often you practice, the greater access you will have to this ability to be present in challenging situations.

Suggested times for the Self-Connection Process:

- Planned times you set aside each day, such as first thing in the morning
- During transitions between activities, for instance as you prepare for a meeting
- During activities throughout the day
- When you are experiencing intensity

EXERCISE

1. BREATH

a. Focus attention on your breathing, while increasing your in-breath and extending your out-breath longer than your in-breath.

2. BODY

a. As you continue to breathe in this way, focus your attention on your body. Bring yourself more fully into your experience by:

   (1) Feeling what you are feeling as you scan all parts of your body, without talking to yourself about what you are feeling. Just experience the sensations.

   (2) Next, talking to yourself about the sensations you are experiencing. For example: "I have discomfort in my shoulders, and buzzing energy in my stomach, etc."

   (3) Then naming what you are feeling. For example: "I am feeling exhilarated," or "I am feeling sad."

3. NEEDS

a. Finally, ask yourself, "When I have this feeling, what need of mine is the nonverbal part of myself signaling is met or not met?" As you suggest needs to yourself in answer to this question, pay attention to the sensations in your body that signal that you have correctly named the need.

b. With this need in mind, imagine what your felt experience would be like if the need were completely met.

c.   Ask yourself, "How can I get this need met now and in the future?"*

*Note: By doing 3b and 3c, you have given your brain a way to work "behind the scenes" to strategize how to get that need met. This is similar to how people can create thoughts that lead to depression by asking questions like, "Why did I screw up?" rather than, "How can I do this better next time?" If I ask "why" in this context, I will get an answer from the brain and it will probably reflect my core beliefs of inadequacy and deficiency. Whereas, if I ask "how," I set the mind to looking for solutions that are likely to generate hope. "How" typically puts you into action, whereas "why" tends to stall you into perseverating on a self-judgment that keeps you from taking action. You can use this tendency to your advantage in asking how to meet the need and imagining it being met.

Part II

Applying the Foundations to Conversation

In Part I, you learned how to tell when you're not connected with yourself and effectively reconnect. We start there because being connected to yourself is helpful to be able to connect with other people. Feelings and needs are the bases for connection with yourself and others; when you can inquire about and recognize your own feelings and needs, it becomes second nature to start guessing what other people might be feeling and needing.

In Part II, we'll start applying these foundational skills when you're interacting with other people. Listening comes first; in order to collaborate with others, you first have to listen to them and demonstrate your understanding. Since teamwork often requires asking for things, we will cover what makes up a request and how to ask in a way that is more likely to meet your needs. In any good team, there may also be disagreements and dissent about the best way forward, leading to difficult conversations. The remainder of Part II will address how to prepare for these conversations, stay present during them, and debrief afterward so that you can learn from what happened and approach the next conversation better equipped to meet your needs.

Listening and Being Listened To

Most people "listen" to others while actually thinking already about what they want to say. Listening, in the way that is referred to here, is first about being present in the moment. It also includes being connected to the person you are listening to by being curious about understanding what they are saying and what needs they are seeking to meet.

By demonstrating your understanding of another's feelings and needs in that moment, you give the other person a sense of being fully heard. One way to demonstrate this is to verbalize your understanding of what they are saying, *perhaps even guessing their needs*. Another way is through nonverbal sounds of understanding and engagement with what they are saying. You can also ask questions for clarification that show you have been paying attention. All of these collectively refer to what we call "empathy."

This process often helps the person who is speaking to you regain connection with themselves and others. It also typically helps them gain understanding about what their needs are in this situation, what they imagine would meet their needs, and what happened to create the situation they are talking about.

For practice purposes, the process of empathizing with another person is broken down into four elements, or stages.

The Four Elements of Empathy

1. **Presence**: Resting your attention on the speaker, not thinking about what is being said or how you are going to respond, and practicing being present.

2. **Silent Empathy**: Silently guessing the meaning of what is being said, including the speaker's Observations, Feelings, Needs, and Requests. More generally put, this element is about guessing silently what is important to the speaker.

3. **Understanding**: Saying what you are hearing back to the speaker in a way that supports them to feel heard about their perspective in the way that you guess they would like to be heard. It is important to clearly indicate you are not agreeing or disagreeing with what they are saying or indicating that what they are saying is objectively true, but rather that you are hearing how they are seeing things from their subjective frame of reference. You may be reflecting back some of their thoughts, but you do so by naming the thoughts as thoughts, which turns them into observations.

4. **Needs**: Guessing what needs might be motivating the speaker, even when that person has not verbalized those needs. At times, this might mean guessing what needs the speaker is seeking to meet by speaking. For instance, when a person talks about a challenge at work, your guess might be, "Are you frustrated because you would like more collaboration in your team?" Be aware of "faux feelings" and translate them into words that name a bodily sensation or feeling. Once the speaker has clarified their needs, you may want to encourage them to take a few moments more to linger on their needs. Finally, you may want to support the person to determine if they have any requests, of themselves or of someone else.

EXERCISE

Version 1—Partner A listens to Partner B, as B talks about something that is important to him or her. Partner A practices the four elements of empathy as follows:

1. Presence: Practice being present for 1 minute

2. Silent Empathy for 1 minute

3. Understanding for 2 minutes

4. Needs for 2 minutes

Version 2—Partner A listens to Partner B, as B talks about something that is important to her or him.

1. Alternate between Presence and Silent Empathy for 2 minutes

2. Alternate between Understanding and Needs for 4 minutes

Debrief:

1. Partner B reports how they felt during the exercise, relating what Partner A said or did to how it prompted them to feel. Reporting on feelings is a way of measuring the connection between you and the effectiveness of Partner A's responses at creating connection.

2. If Partner A would like to provide additional feedback, first ask if Partner B welcomes this kind of feedback.

Repeat: After debriefing, reverse roles and begin again.

The elements are presented here as four steps you practice sequentially. As you become experienced in this type of listening, you will find that you use these elements as reminders when you are listening to another person, and not as steps you go through in sequence.

When conversing "in the wild" (that is, in your business and personal life, as opposed to in a workshop setting), practice presence as much as possible throughout the conversation, as it is the foundation for the other elements of empathy. With that foundation, then moment by moment you might choose one of the other elements based on your evaluation of what will create connection. It's like playing jazz—you have the possibilities available to you with silent empathy, understanding, and needs, as well as all the other strategies for creating connection such as storytelling, humor, advice, play, and any others you know, and you weave them together as you navigate the conversation.

When you are connected to another person, asking for what you'd like or helping them ask for what they'd like becomes much easier. Still, knowing *how* to make a request is essential to being effective in a team. Next, we'll take a look at what requests are and how to make them.

Making Requests

Have you ever left a meeting unclear about the outcome or next steps? Or had a miscommunication with a boss or subordinate about a task? Making requests forms a backdrop of many team interactions, and yet few people are aware of how to be clear in their requests, leading to a significant amount of miscommunication and conflict in the workplace.

In these pages, I will differentiate among **Three Types of Requests.** Common to all three is that they are *requests* and not *demands*. What's the difference?

- Demand: explicitly or implicitly threatens physical or emotional consequences if the person doesn't do what is being demanded.
- Request: asks a person to do something that you are hoping will meet your needs, but also, very important, will meet their needs.

Here are the three types of requests:

Action Requests are asking for a change in behavior, either from another person or from yourself. These are the requests that, if met, you imagine will meet your needs. For example, "Would you be willing to get me a glass of water?" or "Would you tell me your thoughts on the proposal?" or "Would you be able to have the report on my desk by 5 p.m. Friday?"

Process Requests: These two types of requests ask people to tell you either what they have just heard you say, or how they feel having heard what you just said.

1. When you ask people to tell you what they heard you say, you are assessing whether what you communicated was understood as you intended it to be. This request might sound like "Would you be willing to let me know what you just heard me say?"

2. When you ask people to tell you how they feel having heard what you said, you are in a sense seeking to measure the quality of the connection between you. For instance, you learn a lot from people saying that they feel confused compared with saying they feel thankful. This request might sound like "How do you feel having heard that?" or "What's going on for you now that you've heard me?"

Requests have the following characteristics. They are:

1. **Doable,** meaning that they are specific and everyone will know whether the request has been fulfilled. For example, "Will you be more considerate?" is not doable, but "When you finish with your coffee mug would you put it in the dishwasher?" is a doable request.

2. Phrased in the **present tense** to say what you want to happen now. For example, even if you're asking for something that is in the future, such as a report to be completed by Friday, you're still asking for the person's present intention to have it done by then. "Would you be willing to have the report completed by Friday 5 p.m.?"

3. Expressed using **actionable language**, meaning you state what you want, not what you don't want. For example,

"Would you stop interrupting me?" is what you don't want, but to state it in action language, "Will you please allow me to finish what I'm saying?"

Checklist: Suggestions for formulating a request. Ask yourself:
- Is it doable?
- Is it in action language?
- Is it present tense?
- Is it stated as a request, not a demand?

Action requests lead to three kinds of agreements: **Primary, Supporting, and Restoring agreements.**

1. **The Primary agreement** is the focus of the initial request. It is the agreement that once made is the one the parties generally perceive as the central agreement about what is to be done by whom and by when. After completing your new primary agreement, you may want to create supporting or restoring agreements.

2. **Supporting agreements** support doing the primary agreement. Once you have reached a primary agreement, you may want to ask, "Can we make additional agreements that will increase the likelihood that each of us will do what we agreed to do in the primary agreement?

3. **Restoring agreements** may be used if the primary agreement is not kept. You might ask, "If one of us does not do what was agreed to in the primary agreement, what will we do then?" For your restoring agreement, use an "If . . . then . . ." statement. For example, "If one of us does not follow through on the primary agreement, then we will . . ." These agreements might include both actions taken and also how you agree to treat yourselves and each other.

The Consequences of Demands

One of Marshall Rosenberg's enduring insights is that you can force people to do what you want, *but not for the reasons you want them to do it*. When you make a request, you are asking the person to both do what you request and also for them to do it for reasons (needs) that satisfy them.

It may seem that this takes too long. Why, for instance, when you are talking with someone who reports to you in the workplace, can they not just do what you tell them to do? And in some work environments, this is the agreement. For instance, when firefighters go to a fire there is just one fire captain, and the other firefighters at the fire do what they are told. But even in this situation, firefighters are responsible for their safety and the safety of others and thus will question an instruction from the fire captain that unnecessarily endangers lives. Also, even in work situations like this, typically there are mechanisms to review and debrief in order to learn for next time.

If you're concerned that it may take longer to make requests instead of demands, ask yourself, "Will taking this time now save time later?" Generally, there will be undesired consequences that result from making demands. Do you want the person to just do what you say, or do you also want them to have buy-in to what they are doing? Do you want to be part of a collaborative team? If so, then consider whether requesting, instead of demanding, will get you more of what you want.

There are times when you choose to use physical or emotional force. An easy example is when a two-year-old is about to run into the street, and you act by physically bringing the child back to safety. You do not have a conversation about their needs and yours before you act, though you may have that conversation after they are safe.

If you have concluded that you are going to demand your way (rather than make a request), try asking yourself the following questions first:

- Is there any way other than the demand that I can think of to meet my needs and the needs of the other person or persons?

- If there is no other way, am I clear that I am not acting out of anger or the desire to punish?
- Am I willing to make amends later, or live with the disconnection that may result?

A Final Note About Requests

One of the curious things about requests is that you cannot know if you are making a request ahead of time. You can be as clear as possible before making the request and use language that signals you are seeking to make a request, but you only know for sure after you have made it and notice how you respond to receiving a no. You know you really made a demand if you react by trying to coerce the other person to do what you want, either physically or emotionally, such as by inducing shame, guilt, or the threat of punishment.

Preparing for a Difficult Conversation

A difficult conversation is any interaction that *you perceive* to be difficult. There may be a person in your team whom you seem to always butt heads with or simply misunderstand each other. You may be anxious in particular situations, such as asking for a raise or a conversation following a blunder. What often makes a difficult conversation even more difficult is the judgments in place—of you, the other person, or the situation.

People typically hold in their minds a cluster of judgments about another person and concoct stories with those judgments that block them from actually seeing the person accurately. When they have these kinds of judgments, they have less influence with that person, because these thoughts "leak" through how they hold themselves and move, their tone of voice, and their choice of words. There is no way to stop this from happening, and the other person picks up on the subtle cues being sent, receiving the message of disapproval, even if not consciously.

These types of thoughts, or what we call "Enemy Images," make it more challenging to feel a sense of connection with or to feel care and compassion toward another person. They prevent people from recognizing their common humanity.

When you create negative images of others based on critical thoughts of them as wrong, bad, and perhaps deserving to be punished, you not only disconnect yourself from them, but typically these judgments stimulate unpleasant feelings within you. You may feel bitterness, resentment, anger, or even hatred. As you hold these enemy images, *you* suffer, and you also become much less effective in responding to others and the situation in skillful ways that are more likely to meet your needs.

Generally, people tend to create enemy images out of negative judgments. However, you can also have enemy images created out of positive judgments. For instance, people may feel resentful when they put someone on a pedestal. People are also under the influence of enemy images when they are around a cultural icon and become nervous, tongue tied, and generally ill at ease. In this case the judgments are positive, but these thoughts nonetheless disconnect them from the other person.

By dispelling enemy images, you are able to be more present, and thus more effective, in the midst of a difficult conversation. The process below, the Enemy Image Process, will help you transform those enemy images so you can be present and connected.

EXERCISE

This exercise can be done with a practice partner or by yourself through journaling or internal reflection. If you're working with a practice partner, set up your session using the Flight Simulator guidelines on pages 60–62. Partner A talks about the situation he or she would like to gain clarity about. Partner B's role is to support Partner A through the parts of the process, finding the observations, feelings, and needs.

PART I

Empathize With Yourself

1. Observations of:
    a. What the other said or did that triggered your reaction
    b. Judgments, "enemy images," "stories" you have about the other

2. Feelings: Sensations and emotions in your body. Be clear you are naming feelings and not "faux feelings."

3. Needs: Your universal human desires, not specific to any "strategy." Take time to feel and experience the feelings and needs in your body.

Cycling: As you go through the steps, you may notice you have more reaction in you with which to empathize. Continue to cycle through steps 1–3 until you feel complete for the moment, connected to your needs, and feeling a degree of inner calm, relaxation, and centeredness.

PART II

Empathize With Other

In this step, you connect within yourself to the other person's experience:

1. Observations of:
   a. What you said or did that might have been triggering to the other
   b. What their thoughts about you and the situation might be

2. Feelings: What the other person might be feeling, what sensations and emotions they may be experiencing in their body.

3. Needs: What might be their universal human needs, not specific to any "strategy."

Cycling: As you move through these steps, continue cycling through all three until you feel complete for the moment, connected to the other, more peaceful and nonreactive. Also, as you attempt to empathize with the other, you may get triggered into more of your own reactions. If this happens, go back to Part I and cycle back and forth between Part I and Part II as needed.

PART III

Emergence of New Possibilities to Meet Needs

Ask yourself about your:

1. Learning from doing Parts 1 and 2. Any new ideas, insights, or possibilities that have emerged that you now see?

2. Plan of action for how to meet your needs now that you are on the "other side of connection." See if you can form specific, action-language, "doable" requests of yourself or other people.

3. Practice: After forming an action request and a plan, you may want to practice whatever you came up with. If this involves a conversation, you can practice what you might actually say; and also practice dealing with challenging ways the other person might respond. Ways to do this include role-playing a practice conversation with a coach or practice partner, or through journaling.

Cycling: As you go through these steps, you may notice more conflict reactions coming up in you. You could then go back to Parts I and II, and cycle back and forth between Parts I and II and Part III until you feel ready to complete Part III.

Any time you know you will be in a difficult conversation, use the process above to take care of any enemy images you have of yourself or the other person to prepare for the conversation. Sometimes, you won't know that a conversation will be difficult, and you'll be in the midst of it when you find that you're triggered and in the stress response. At that point, you can ask to take a time-out to reconnect to yourself and return to the conversation later, or simply finish the conversation and regroup from there, using the Debriefing for Resilience process on pages 41–46.

You can also practice in such a way that the same situations do not trigger you as easily, and that's the practice we'll turn to next.

Practicing Difficult Conversations

Have you ever been in a situation with people who irritate you, vowed to never let them irritate you again, only to find yourself later in the same reactive pattern? The things that trigger you are likely based in behavioral habits that began in childhood, yet they can be changed. The exercise in this section will help desensitize you to triggering conversations.

It can be used for several purposes; you can use it for a conversation that you anticipate will be challenging for you, and you can also use it to learn from a conversation you had that you would like to revisit.

As you revisit conversations from the past or imagine conversations you anticipate, you learn what the early stages of the Fight-Flight-Freeze response feel like. By doing so, you will be more skilled at becoming aware when you start to be triggered. With this early warning, you will be able to choose to do something like the Self-Connection Process to return to presence, and thus reduce the load of stress hormones in your system.

Also, you will train using your communication skills in simulated real situations. You will get to practice responding in alignment with your values when you are "feeling" the stress.

EXERCISE

Find a partner to practice with and set up your practice session using the Flight Simulator on pages 60–62. Agree with your partner who is going to go first with their scenario (Partner A).

1. Partner A first tells Partner B:

    a. Their relationship to the person they are asking Partner B to role-play. For instance, "I would like you to play a colleague at work" or "I'd like you to be someone that reports to me" or "You're going to play my boss" or "You're one of my customers."

b. Their "trigger." This is what Partner B is being asked to say or do in order to provide the trigger to Partner A.

From Step 2 on, "you" corresponds to Partner A:

2. Check in to see if you want to do the Self-Connection Process before starting.

a. Bringing a difficult scenario to mind and telling it to your practice partner may trigger the stress response. Remember you can do the Self-Connection Process out loud and you can ask Partner B to help you by guessing your feelings and needs. Whether you ask for your partner to empathize with you is your choice.

3. Tell your partner you are ready for them to deliver the trigger. Ask your partner to start with a low-level of intensity and gradually raise it.

4. Stop your partner by raising your hand when you notice the first flickering of the stress response.

5. Do your Self-Connection Process out loud, so your partner will know what is going on. If you would like, ask your partner to support you by empathizing with you.

6. After doing the Self-Connection Process and having some sense of having returned to presence, ask yourself, "Can I hear the message (the trigger) as a 'please' or 'thank you'?"

7. Next, decide how you plan to respond, either by Empathizing or by Self-Expressing. Tell your partner which you plan to practice.

a. If you choose to empathize, remember the four elements of empathy—presence, silent empathy, understanding, needs.

   (1) If you would like, you can use this empathy template: "Are you ＿＿ [FEELINGS] because you want ＿＿ [NEEDS]?"

b. If you choose to self-express, you can use the following template:

   (1) "When I see/hear you ＿＿ [OBSERVATION], I feel ＿＿ [FEELINGS], because I want ＿＿ [NEEDS].

   (2) End your expression with either
     (a) An action request, e.g., "Would you tell me ＿＿?"
     (b) A connection request: e.g., "How do you feel hearing this?" or "Would you tell me what you are hearing me say?"

8. In response to your empathy guess or to your self-expression, Partner B delivers a second trigger, which will be some version of the first trigger.

a. In response to this trigger, respond with either empathizing or expressing, whichever you did not do in response to the first request.

b. Repeat from Step 3 as desired.

c. When you are satisfied with doing the exercise with the first person, then both partners "de-role," which means to pause, and in some way to acknowledge to your partner and your partner to you that you have stopped the role-play, that you are no longer playing a role, and that you are now your own self interacting with your partner.

9. Debrief:

   a. Ask your partner to tell you how they felt while hearing your empathy or expression. This is a way of measuring how connecting what you said was.

   b. Report how you felt during the process.

   c. If your partner would like to provide additional feedback, we suggest that first they ask you if this kind of feedback is welcomed by you before providing it.

10. After doing the exercise once or twice, playing these roles, reverse roles and begin again with the second partner's scenario.

Practicing the skills of reconnecting to yourself and responding to the other person with empathy or self-expression are invaluable tools for being in conversation in the workplace. Regardless of your level of skill, however, conversations always give opportunities to keep learning and growing. The best way to take advantage of these opportunities is to reflect on your conversations—to do a debrief.

Debriefing for Resilience

In many workplace situations, a debrief is built into the workflow—people take the time after a campaign or event to assess how things went and what might have gone better. Yet most people don't do this in situations that matter most, interactions with those people closest to them. If you take a look at what went well and what you'd like to improve, you set yourself up to be in a continuous process of learning. However, how you do this debrief makes all the difference.

The process we suggest is a way of debriefing which of your needs *were not* met (mourning) and which *were met* (celebrating) in an interaction. It can be practiced on your own (silently or by journaling), or you can go through it with another person's support. In either case, the process proceeds by making a series of guesses, either to yourself or to you by your partner. If with yourself, you guess what needs were met or not met, and let your body's reaction (how you feel) tell you whether you have accurately identified the need met or not met. If you are supported by a partner, the partner not only guesses your needs met or not met but may also ask you questions that are intended to support you in being clearer about your reflection.

EXERCISE

If you are practicing with a partner, set up your session using the Flight Simulator on pages 60–62, and agree who is going to go first with their scenario.

PART I: MOURN
Empathize with yourself, so as to discern which of your needs were *not met* by what happened in a situation you are reflecting upon. Or, if you are working with a practice partner, he or she can support you in this process by making guesses using the following outline.

1. Observations: Bring to mind the situation.

    a. What happened that did not meet your needs? What was said or done?

    b. Do you have any negative thoughts, judgments, or stories about this? If so, sort through them to identify the observations, that is, what was actually said or done that did not meet your needs.

2. Feelings: With your observations in your mind, pay attention to the sensations and emotions in your body. As you do this, name these feelings.

3. Needs: Identify the needs that the nonverbal part of your brain expresses as not being met through your thoughts and feelings.

Cycling: Move through the three steps in whatever order works for you. Continue to cycle through the steps until you feel inner calm, which you can use as a sign of being connected to your needs.

PART II: CELEBRATE
Empathize with yourself or have your practice partner support you by guessing which of your needs were met by what happened in the conversation or interaction.

1. Observations

    a. What happened that met your needs, including things that might happen in the future as a result of what occurred?

2. Feelings: Sensations and emotions in your body—name them.

3. Needs: Identify the needs that the nonverbal part of your brain expresses as being met through your thoughts and feelings.

Cycling: As with Part I, you may cycle through the steps multiple times. Also, as you are in Part II, you many also notice more thoughts and feelings relating to unmet needs coming up. At any point you can cycle back to Part I, and back and forth between Parts I and II.

PART III:
Emergence of new possibilities for similar situations in the future

1.   **Learning from Parts I and II:** What new ideas, insights, or possibilities do you now see? What did you learn from doing Parts I and II?

2.   **Plan of action:** With what you have learned in mind, what ideas, if any, occur to you regarding what you would like to do to be better prepared for similar situations in the future? Is there a skill you would like to practice? Do you have a plan to re-engage with the people who were part of the situation you worked with? Do you have a request of yourself or anyone else?

3.   **Practice:** After forming an action request and a plan, you may want to practice the skills you will need in similar situations in the future. One way to do this is to role-play a practice conversation with a practice partner or coach, or to journal imagined future situations.

Cycling: After reaching Step 3, you may notice you have more learning and insights. If so, you can cycle back through the steps. You might also notice more coming up to empathize with about needs met and/or not met. If so, you can go back to Parts I and II.

Debrief after each person in the following way:

1.   The person who just mourned and celebrated starts by saying how it was for them, how they felt at different points during the exercise.

2. The practice partner then says how it was for them.

3. Next, the focus shifts back to whether the person who mourned and celebrated has any requests for specific feedback from their practice partner.

4. Finally, the focus shifts back to the practice partner. At that point, if the practice partner has suggestions regarding how the person who mourned and celebrated might have done it differently, then this is the time for the practice partner to ask if this kind of feedback is desired.

As you grow more comfortable with this process of mourning needs not met and celebrating the needs that were met, you may want to include this as a regular part of your team's processes. When doing this with your team, you may want to start by asking, "What worked?" This is a way to start looking for what happened (the "observations") that met the needs of one or more team members. This will help you and your team to shift out of judging what took place and instead appreciate the needs that were met. When you and your team feel complete with this, you can then turn to what needs were not met. It is generally helpful to start with what worked as opposed to what did not. This will build trust that what is being sought are needs and not judgments or criticisms.

Learning Cycle

When learning from a conflict conversation, shifting the focus to meeting needs changes how you are in the world. Most people have been taught how to think and evaluate in terms of blame and punishment, which leads to seeking to avoid these. By focusing only on avoiding what you do not want, you end up not learning new, more adaptive behaviors but instead perpetuate old habits. This exercise provides an alternative cycle. First you do something, then assess how needs were met or not met. Finally, you learn from this how to move toward what you want—how to better meet needs in the future.

Part III

Further Collaboration Applications

You now know the basic skills to stay connected with yourself and other people, even in the midst of challenging situations, and continue to learn from those conversations to better meet your own and others' needs. Working in teams provides a few additional situations in which having these skills helps you navigate the conversation more successfully: when you . . .

- Need to interrupt someone
- Hear a no to your request, or are turning down someone else's request
- Have feedback to give to someone on your team
- Would like to express appreciation to someone

In this section, we'll cover each of these scenarios, showing how you can practice your skills and stay connected to needs throughout.

Interrupting

Though most people have been taught that it's rude to interrupt, in fact interruption can be a critical tool in many interactions, especially in helping to keep meetings focused. This is typically not interrupting to be heard yourself, its intention is to meet the needs of everyone. When the interrupter uses this strategy to clarify their understanding of what they are hearing, it also helps the speaker to be heard the way they want to be heard and communicate as they intend.

Being clear about what need you are seeking to meet before you begin to interrupt will aid you in being connected with the person you are interrupting. Doing so will also help you to use fewer words, which is generally a plus.

Examples of situations when you might want to interrupt to meet not only your needs but also the needs of the person you are interrupting include when you want to:

- Demonstrate that you have heard the other person
- Clarify your understanding of some part of what has been said
- Stick to the agreed agenda (or change it)
- Engage with someone who is using more words than you would like

Thus, you may want to do the Self-Connection Process with a few breaths before you interrupt. This is because when you interrupt you want to let the speaker know as soon as possible what need you are seeking to meet by interrupting. And as quickly as possible, you want to end your interruption with a request. So, for example, you might say: "Excuse me, excuse me, I really want to understand what you are saying. Would you tell me a summary of what you are saying in twenty-five words or less?"

Tips for Interrupting:

- Pause long enough to be sure you know what you are going to say before you start to interrupt.
- When you do start to interrupt,
  - Reveal your need (why you are interrupting) in as few words as possible and as early on as possible.
  - Make a request in as few words as possible.
  - Gain the other person's attention by saying something like: "Excuse me, excuse me. . . ."

■ Be careful how you use your hands when you interrupt

- For instance, holding your palm facing the other person may not be well received.

EXERCISE

1. With your practice partner, decide who is going to be the "Speaker" and who is going to be the "Interrupter."

2. The Interrupter tells the Speaker:

    a. The relationship between the Interrupter and the person the Speaker is role-playing, for example, "You are going to play my coworker."

    b. The Interrupter next tells the Speaker what they want them to say as part of the role-play.

3. The Speaker then begins speaking and, as he or she does so, the Interrupter silently determines what need they hope will be met by interrupting and formulates the request they will make of the Speaker.

4. The Interrupter then interrupts and says what they have planned to say.

5. After the interruption, stop, go out of roles, and debrief.

6. During the debrief:

    a. The Interrupter asks the Speaker to report how they felt as a result of being interrupted. Asking the Speaker to report how they felt is a way of measuring the connection between the Speaker and the Interrupter.

b. The Interrupter then reports how they felt during the process of preparing to interrupt and actually interrupting.

c. If the Speaker would like to provide additional feedback, first ask if the Interrupter welcomes this kind of feedback.

d. After repeating the exercise two or three times playing these roles, reverse roles and begin again.

The Need Behind the No

What's your typical reaction when you hear a no after making a request? For many people, it may be anger or frustration and lead to conflict with the other person. Yet, there's a way to hear a no that allows you to stay in connection and communication with the person, and still aim to meet your needs and theirs. Similarly, when your response to someone else's request is a no, this process will help you in the same way.

If you are making a request and receive anything other than an unambiguous yes, clarify the need that the other person is saying yes to, when they are saying no to you. One way to refer to this is to look for the need behind the no.

If you are the one receiving the request and you are saying anything other than an unambiguous yes, communicate the need you are saying yes to when you are saying no to the other person.

In both these situations, follow by making a request that is intended on your part to meet both the other person's needs and yours. This will lead you into a conversation in which you can collaborate in meeting the needs of both. This kind of request will tend to avoid a conflict and support more connection.

Let's take an example and show the need behind the no from both perspectives: receiving a request and making one.

Your colleague asks you if you can help him with a project by editing the report he's about to submit. You don't want to do it, but rather than simply saying no, you respond in a way that connects him to your needs, saying something like, "I'd really like to help, and right now I'm feeling time-pressured to meet the deadline on the project that I'm working on. Is there someone else you'd be willing to ask to review your report?"

Alternatively, if you were the one asking for the editing help and your colleague responds, "No way, I can't," you might want to look for the need behind your colleague's no by asking, "Is that because you are time-pressured on your own project?" If, on the other hand, your colleague responded by saying, "No way, I'm barely going to get my own project in on time," he has colloquially provided you with his need behind the no.

It often happens that you can discern a person's need behind their no. However, when it is not clear to you what is motivating their refusal, you can use these tools to look for their need. The benefit of this is that it helps nurture connection; where otherwise you might feel hurt or disconnected (since hearing no often brings up rejection), when you clarify the need that the other person is meeting by saying it you understand why they are turning down your request.

EXERCISE

1. Agree with your partner who is going to go first with their scenario (Partner A).

2. Partner A tells Partner B the relationship between Partner A and the person Partner B is role-playing, for example, "You are going to play my boss."

3. Let Partner B know whether you are practicing the need behind the no making a request or receiving a request.

a. If you are practicing making a request, Partner B's role is to respond with no, and then in role respond to your empathy and subsequent requests.

b. If you are practicing receiving a request, let Partner B know what request they are making of you.

When you are making the request:

1. Practice the Self-Connection Process out loud so your partner is included.

2. Make your request and in so doing reveal the need that you are hoping will be met.

3. Partner B responds with no.

4. Empathize with the need behind Partner B's no.

5. After Partner B responds to the empathy, make another request that attempts to reconcile the needs of both parties.

6. If Partner B's response is anything other than an unqualified yes, continue to empathize and search for a request that reconciles the needs of both parties until an agreement is reached.

7. Go out of role and debrief.

Debrief:

1. Partner A reports how they felt during the exercise making the request and empathizing.

2. Partner B relates how they felt during the exercise, connecting specific observations with how they felt at that point in the exercise.

3. If Partner B would like to provide suggestions about how Partner A might have said or done something differently, first ask your practice partner if this kind of feedback is welcome.

When you are receiving the request:

1. Practice the Self-Connection Process out loud so your partner is included and let Partner B know when you're ready to begin.

2. Partner B makes the request.

3. Empathize with the needs behind the request being made of you and while doing so, also clarify the request.

4. Communicate the needs behind your no.

5. Search for a request that reconciles the needs of both parties.

6. Continue the conversation until an agreement emerges.

Debrief:

1. Partner A reports how they felt during the exercise.

2. Partner B relates how they felt during the exercise, connecting specific observations with how they felt at that point in the exercise.

3. If Partner B would like to provide suggestions about how Partner A might have said or done something differently, first ask if this kind of feedback is welcome.

Giving (and Receiving) Feedback

Both giving and receiving feedback are essential to learning and growing in both business and personal lives. It is from feedback that you gain the critical information from which you can change and grow. That being said, it is often difficult to receive feedback and to give feedback that is welcomed by the receiver. The key in both situations is to stay focused on the quality of your connection with the other person and with yourself. The moment you discern disconnection, it is important to focus on re-creating and strengthening that connection. If there is no connection, the speaker is not likely to be understood as she or he would like to be.

The following are reasons to focus on the quality of connection while giving and receiving feedback:

1. If I am disconnected from myself, it makes it more difficult for me
   a. to take in and learn from feedback, and
   b. to give the kind of feedback that will be easily received.
2. If I am connected to myself, I will likely be more able to take in your feedback, no matter how disconnected you are from yourself and me, and how judgmentally the feedback is given.
3. If you and I are disconnected, it is highly unlikely that you will be able to take in the feedback I offer, no matter how well intentioned.

When formulating your feedback, if you are clear about your Observations, Feelings, Needs, and Requests, you are likely to find that the person to whom you are giving the feedback will find it easier to take it in. Tell the person your observation in order to orient them to what you are going to say next. For example, saying, "When you gave me the report at the end of the day yesterday, and we had agreed that you would give it to me at 10 a.m. in time for my meeting with my sales manager . . .," orients your listener to what you are talking about. If you do it as an observation rather than a judgment, they are more likely to continue to listen.

The typical detriment of using a judgment is the person's internal processes begin to defend against the judgment. Judgments typically act to disconnect the listener from whatever you say next. Keeping this in mind, be very clear about the observation, without inserting any sense of judgment.

Now, you cannot prevent a person from hearing your observation as a judgment, particularly if, as in this example, the person receiving the feedback may already have a sense of judgment about "missing a deadline." Nonetheless, you can do your part by orienting your listener by starting with an observation. Then you use your current feeling and needs (met and not met) in order to connect them to you and to increase the likelihood that they will be receptive to your request.

So, for instance, "When I think about you giving your report to me after my sales meeting instead of before, as we agreed, I'm frustrated because I want us to work as a team and I need your support. I'd like to understand what was going on with you so that you didn't get the report to me before my meeting. Would you tell me what happened?"

In this example, the feedback concerns something that the speaker did not like in the behavior of the person to whom they are giving the feedback. When providing feedback to a person about something that person did that you liked, it is expressing appreciation, which will be covered in the next section.

EXERCISE

With your practice partner, decide who is going to give and who is going to receive feedback.

1. The "Giver" tells the "Receiver" the relationship between the Giver and the person the Receiver is role-playing, for example, "You are going to play my coworker Sara."

2. The Giver takes a moment to silently reflect on the scenario she or he is imagining and formulates the proposed feedback. The Giver can draw upon real-life experience they want to practice as a "do-over" or they can imagine something that they foresee doing in the future.

3. Pause at this moment so that both the "Giver" and the "Receiver" have the opportunity to do the Self-Connection Process if they wish.

4. Agree to start.

5. At this point, the Giver delivers the feedback to the Receiver.

6. The Receiver takes in the feedback but does not respond verbally to the Giver. Instead, they take a moment to imagine what they would like to say and remember it for the debrief.

7. Stop, go out of roles, and debrief.

8. During the debrief:

    a. The Giver asks the Receiver to tell how they felt as a result of hearing the feedback. Asking the Receiver to report how they felt is a way of measuring the connection between the Giver and the Receiver.

    b. The Giver then reports how they felt during the process of giving the feedback.

    c. If the Giver would like to receive additional feedback, including perhaps what the Receiver might have said in response to the feedback, this is the time for the Giver to ask for it.

> d. If the Receiver would like to provide additional feedback, first ask if this kind of feedback is welcomed by the Giver.
>
> 9. After repeating the exercise two or three times playing these roles, reverse roles and begin again.

The preceding exercise focuses on the Giver practicing how to give feedback that is more easily received. Receiving feedback may come in a form that is triggering for you, or in some cases it's not triggering, but it just isn't clear or helpful. If it's a trigger and you've moved into the Fight-Flight-Freeze response, use the Practicing Difficult Conversations exercise to develop the capacity to stay present in the face of the trigger of receiving it. If that's not the case, and it's just feedback that's not clear and specific, then simply start at Step 9 of Practicing Difficult Conversations, and use the skills of Self-Empathy and Self-Expression to arrive at clarity about what the person would actually like to communicate.

Expressing Appreciation

At work and in your personal life, there are times when you may want to express your appreciation or gratitude. Key to expressing gratitude or appreciation is distinguishing between your judgment of the other person's conduct and the observation of what they actually said or did that you are appreciating. Therefore, when you express your appreciation, include your observation of what you are appreciating, as well as your need and a request. You may also include how you feel about the observation that you are appreciating; this is optional, though it is often helpful for the person receiving gratitude to understand the fuller impact on you that is prompting you to express your appreciation.

Expressing appreciation might sound something like this:

> "The way you talked to Bob just then on that sales call was very satisfying as I am more trusting that you will be able to handle customer interactions on your own in the future. Do you like hearing that?" (Or "How is that to hear?")

Or

> "I am very satisfied about how you handled that call. As a result, I have more trust that you are ready to handle these calls on your own. Are you pleased with your progress?" (Or "Are you pleased with the call?")

Expressing appreciation or gratitude is a particular type of feedback.

EXERCISE

1. With your practice partner, decide who is going to express appreciation and who is going to receive it.

2. The "Expresser" tells the "Receiver" the relationship between the Expresser and the person the Receiver is role-playing, for example, "You are going to play my customer Peter."

3. The Expresser takes a moment to silently reflect on the scenario she or he is imagining and formulates the proposed expression of appreciation. The Expresser can draw upon real-life experience they want to practice.

4. Pause at this moment so that both the "Expresser" and the "Receiver" have the opportunity to do the Self-Connection Process if they wish.

5. Next, agree to start.

6. At this point, the Expresser voices appreciation to the Receiver by:

   a. Specifically stating the observation of what was said or done that is prompting the expression of appreciation,

   b. How the Expresser is feeling about that observation, and

   c. What need of the Expresser's is met remembering the observation.

7. The Receiver takes in the appreciation but does not respond verbally to the Expresser. Instead, they take a moment to remember how they felt hearing the appreciation and imagine what they might have said in response to it for the debrief.

8. Stop, go out of roles, and debrief.

9. During the debrief:

   a. The Expresser asks the Receiver to report how they felt as a result of hearing the appreciation. Asking the Receiver to report how they felt is a way of measuring the connection between the Expresser and the Receiver.

   b. The Expresser then reports how they felt during the process of expressing the appreciation.

   c. If the Expresser would like to receive additional feedback, including perhaps what the Receiver might have said in response to the appreciation, this is the time for the Expresser to ask for it.

10. After repeating the exercise two or three times playing these roles, reverse roles and begin again.

Expressing appreciation tends to be underrated in the workplace, yet can have powerful impact on people's level of happiness and productivity. Look for opportunities on your team to express your appreciation and see how it changes your relationship to your coworkers and the dynamics of the team in general.

Flight Simulator Practice
Guidelines for Dyad Practice

Practicing the communication skills in this book with a partner is like being in a flight simulator. Pilots learning to fly practice in a simulation of real-life conditions to learn the skills they need, before their own and other people's lives depend on it. Training in simulated situations has now also become cutting edge in other fields where people need to operate effectively while experiencing the stress response, such as first responders, emergency room personnel, and military Special Forces.

Though your relationships and workplaces may not carry the same life-and-death implications, you can use the same principles to more effectively be able to act in interpersonal situations the way you would like.

Flight simulators have the ability to dial the difficulty up and down based on your skill level, and that can be built into your practice too. The point is *not* to see how many times you can crash and burn or how much intensity you can take, but rather to identify the earliest stages of the stress response—giving you more choice in acting to reduce the release of stress hormones—and to learn new skills and ways of being in intense situations. The way to learn effectively is to keep some control over how much stress you experience so that you feel safe and in your optimal learning zone. As you set up and go through any practice with your partner, think about dialing the difficulty up or down as you need to, making requests of your partner as necessary, to be able to practice responding as you would like.

For any of the exercises in this book that you are practicing with another person, use the following to set up and conduct your practice session.

Starting the Practice Session

1. Brief check-in for each of you to say how you are doing. Particularly on days when you or your partner experience some level of stress, communicating this can be important for what you practice and how.
2. See if someone has a real situation that they would like to "put into the chairs." (If not, you can always create a general context, such as a relationship, family, or workplace conflict and create roles out of these contexts.)
3. Decide what scenario you are going to practice with, and what specific skills you would like to work on.

Setting Up the Role-Play

1. Decide who is going to play which role.
2. Tell only enough of the story to get the role-play started. No need to tell the whole story. Much of the story will come out during the role-play.
3. Dial the difficulty so as to remain in the learning zone.
4. Confirm any agreements you want to have about confidentiality.
5. If either of you are stimulated by, for instance, talking about something that is triggering for you, then do the Self-Connection Process. If you're willing, do it out loud to include your partner in what is going on and so your partner can support you getting to your needs.

Options During the Role-Play
(In the "Flight Simulator")

1. Pause the role-play to do the Self-Connection Process, out loud (or silently).
2. Pause and consider out loud your options.
3. Pause and ask your partner for their feedback.

4. Pause and ask your practice partner to dial the difficulty up or down.
5. Rewind and do over what you want to practice.

After the Role-Play

(Debriefing and Feedback)

1. Each person provides "bio-feedback," meaning each tells the other person how he or she felt at particular moments. Make this as specific as possible, i.e., "When you reflected my needs after I said . . ., I felt relief."
2. Ask if any other kind of feedback is welcome before providing it.
3. After feedback, switch so the second person can work on one of their scenarios.

Appendix: Faux Feelings

FAUX FEELING	FEELING(S)	NEED(S)
Abandoned	Terrified, hurt, bewildered, sad, frightened, lonely	Nurturing, connection, belonging, support, caring
Abused	Angry, frustrated, frightened	Caring, nurturing, support, emotional or physical well-being, consideration, need for all living things to flourish
(Not) accepted	Upset, scared, lonely	Inclusion, connection, community, belonging, contribution, peer respect
Attacked	Scared, angry	Safety
Belittled	Angry, frustrated, tense, distressed	Respect, autonomy, to be seen, acknowledgment, appreciation
Betrayed	Angry, hurt, disappointed, enraged	Trust, dependability, honesty, honor, commitment, clarity
Blamed	Angry, scared, confused, antagonistic, hostile, bewildered, hurt	Accountability, causality, fairness, justice
Bullied	Angry, scared, pressured	Autonomy, choice, safety, consideration
Caged/boxed in	Angry, thwarted, scared, anxious	Autonomy, choice, freedom
Cheated	Resentful, hurt, angry	Honesty, fairness, justice, trust, reliability
Coerced	Angry, frustrated, frightened, thwarted, scared	Choice, autonomy, freedom, act freely, choose freely
Cornered	Angry, scared, anxious, thwarted	Autonomy, freedom
Criticized	In pain, scared, anxious, frustrated, humiliated, angry, embarrassed	Understanding, acknowledgment, recognition, accountability, nonjudgmental communication
Discounted/ Diminished	Hurt, angry, embarrassed, frustrated	Need to matter, acknowledgment, inclusions, recognition, respect
Disliked	Sad, lonely, hurt	Connection, appreciation, understanding, acknowledgment, friendship, inclusion
Distrusted	Sad, frustrated	Trust, honesty
Dumped on	Angry, overwhelmed	Respect, consideration

FAUX FEELING	FEELING(S)	NEED(S)
Harassed	Angry, frustrated, pressured, frightened	Respect, space, consideration, peace
Hassled	Irritated, distressed, angry, frustrated	Serenity, autonomy, do things at my own pace and in my own way, calm, space
Ignored	Lonely, scared, hurt, sad, embarrassed	Connection, belonging, inclusion, community, participation
Insulted	Angry, embarrassed	Respect, consideration, acknowledgment, recognition
Interrupted	Angry, frustrated, resentful, hurt	Respect, to be heard, consideration
Intimidated	Scared, anxiety	Safety, equality, empowerment
Invalidated	Angry, hurt, resentful	Appreciation, respect, acknowledgment, recognition
Invisible	Sad, angry, lonely, scared	To be seen and heard, inclusion, belonging, community
Isolated	Lonely, afraid, scared	Community, inclusion, belonging, contribution
Left out	Sad, lonely, anxious	Inclusion, belonging, community, connection
Let down	Sad, disappointed, frightened	Consistency, trust, dependability, consistency
Manipulated	Angry, scared, powerless, thwarted, frustrated	Autonomy, empowerment, trust, equality, freedom, free choice, connection, genuineness
Mistrusted	Sad, angry	Trust
Misunderstood	Upset, angry, frustrated	To be heard, understanding, clarity
Neglected	Lonely, scared	Connection, inclusion, participation, community, care, mattering, consideration
Overpowered	Angry, impotent, helpless, confused	Equality, justice, autonomy, freedom
Overworked	Angry, tired, frustrated	Respect, consideration, rest, caring
Patronized	Angry, frustrated, resentful	Recognition, equality, respect, mutuality
Pressured	Anxious, resentful, overwhelmed	Relaxation, clarity, space, consideration

FAUX FEELING	FEELING(S)	NEED(S)
Provoked	Angry, frustrated, hostile, antagonistic, resentful	Respect, consideration
Put down	Angry, sad, embarrassed	Respect, acknowledgment, understanding
Rejected	Hurt, scared, angry, defiant	Belonging, inclusion, closeness, to be seen, acknowledgment, connection
Ripped off/screwed	Anger, resentment, disappointment	Consideration, justice, fairness, justice, acknowledgment, trust
Smothered/suffocated	Frustration, fear, desperation	Space, freedom, autonomy, authenticity, self-expression
Taken for granted	Sad, angry, hurt, disappointment	Appreciation, acknowledgment, recognition, consideration
Threatened	Scared, frightened, alarmed, agitated, defiant	Safety, autonomy
Trampled	Angry, frustrated, overwhelmed	Empowerment, connection, community, being seen, consideration, equality, respect, acknowledgment
Tricked	Embarrassed, angry, resentful	Integrity, trust, honesty
Unappreciated	Sad, angry, hurt, frustrated	Appreciation, respect, acknowledgment, consideration
Unheard	Sad, hostile, frustrated	Understanding, consideration, empathy
Unloved	Sad, bewildered, frustrated	Love, appreciation, empathy, connection, community
Unseen	Sad, anxious, frustrated	Acknowledgment, appreciation, be heard
Unsupported	Sad, hurt, resentful	Support, understanding
Unwanted	Sad, anxious, frustrated	Belonging, inclusion, caring
Used	Sad, angry, resentful	Autonomy, equality, consideration, mutuality
Victimized	Frightened, helpless	Empowerment, mutuality, safety, justice
Violated	Sad, agitated, anxiety	Privacy, safety, trust, space, respect
Wronged	Angry, hurt, resentful, irritated	Respect, justice, trust, safety, fairness

* These are selections from a list developed in April 2000 for the Wisconsin International Intensive Training, an NVC workshop, edited by Susan Skye.

Index

The Four-Part Nonviolent Communication Process

Clearly expressing
how **I am**
without blaming
or criticizing

Empathically receiving
how **you are**
without hearing
blame or criticism

OBSERVATIONS

1. What I observe *(see, hear, remember, imagine, free from my evaluations)* that does or does not contribute to my well-being:

   "When I (see, hear) . . . "

1. What you observe *(see, hear, remember, imagine, free from your evaluations)* that does or does not contribute to your well-being:

   "When you see/hear . . . "

   (Sometimes unspoken when offering empathy)

FEELINGS

2. How I feel *(emotion or sensation rather than thought)* in relation to what I observe:

   "I feel . . . "

2. How you feel *(emotion or sensation rather than thought)* in relation to what you observe:

   "You feel . . ."

NEEDS

3. What I need or value *(rather than a preference, or a specific action)* that causes my feelings:

   " . . . because I need/value . . . "

3. What you need or value *(rather than a preference, or a specific action)* that causes your feelings:

   " . . . because you need/value . . ."

Clearly requesting that
which would enrich **my**
life without demanding

Empathically receiving that
which would enrich **your** life
without hearing any demand

REQUESTS

4. The concrete actions I would like taken:

   "Would you be willing to . . . ?"

4. The concrete actions you would like taken:

   "Would you like . . . ?"

   (Sometimes unspoken when offering empathy)

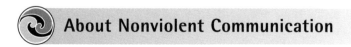

About Nonviolent Communication

Nonviolent Communication has flourished for more than four decades across sixty countries selling more than 1,500,000 books in over thirty languages for one simple reason: it works.

From the bedroom to the boardroom, from the classroom to the war zone, Nonviolent Communication (NVC) is changing lives every day. NVC provides an easy-to-grasp, effective method to get to the root of violence and pain peacefully. By examining the unmet needs behind what we do and say, NVC helps reduce hostility, heal pain, and strengthen professional and personal relationships. NVC is now being taught in corporations, classrooms, prisons, and mediation centers worldwide. And it is affecting cultural shifts as institutions, corporations, and governments integrate NVC consciousness into their organizational structures and their approach to leadership.

Most of us are hungry for skills that can improve the quality of our relationships, to deepen our sense of personal empowerment or simply help us communicate more effectively. Unfortunately, most of us have been educated from birth to compete, judge, demand, and diagnose; to think and communicate in terms of what is "right" and "wrong" with people. At best, the habitual ways we think and speak hinder communication and create misunderstanding or frustration. And still worse, they can cause anger and pain, and may lead to violence. Without wanting to, even people with the best of intentions generate needless conflict.

NVC helps us reach beneath the surface and discover what is alive and vital within us, and how all of our actions are based on human needs that we are seeking to meet. We learn to develop a vocabulary of feelings and needs that helps us more clearly express what is going on in us at any given moment. When we understand and acknowledge our needs, we develop a shared foundation for much more satisfying relationships. Join the thousands of people worldwide who have improved their relationships

About PuddleDancer Press

PuddleDancer Press (PDP) is the main publisher of Nonviolent Communication™ related works. Its mission is to provide high-quality materials to help people create a world in which all needs are met compassionately. By working in partnership with the Center for Nonviolent Communication and NVC trainers, teams, and local supporters, PDP has created a comprehensive promotion effort that has helped bring NVC to thousands of new people each year.

Since 1998 PDP has donated more than 60,000 NVC books to organizations, decision-makers, and individuals in need around the world. **Visit the PDP website at www.NonviolentCommunication.com to find the following resources:**

- **Shop NVC**—Continue your learning. Purchase our NVC titles online safely, affordably, and conveniently. Find everyday discounts on individual titles, multiple-copies, and book packages. Learn more about our authors and read endorsements of NVC from world-renowned communication experts and peacemakers. www.NonviolentCommunication.com/store/

- **NVC Quick Connect e-Newsletter**—Sign up today to receive our monthly e-Newsletter, filled with expert articles, upcoming training opportunities with our authors, and exclusive specials on NVC learning materials. Archived e-Newsletters are also available

- **About NVC**—Learn more about these life-changing communication and conflict resolution skills including an overview of the NVC process, key facts about NVC, and more.

- **About Marshall Rosenberg**—Access press materials, biography, and more about this world-renowned peacemaker, educator, bestselling author, and founder of the Center for Nonviolent Communication.

- **Free Resources for Learning NVC**—Find free weekly tips series, NVC article archive, and other great resources to make learning these vital communication skills just a little easier.

For more information, please contact PuddleDancer Press at:

2240 Encinitas Blvd., Ste. D-911 • Encinitas, CA 92024
Phone: 760-652-5754 • Fax: 760-274-6400
Email: email@puddledancer.com • www.NonviolentCommunication.com

About the Center for Nonviolent Communication

The Center for Nonviolent Communication (CNVC) is an international nonprofit peacemaking organization whose vision is a world where everyone's needs are met peacefully. CNVC is devoted to supporting the spread of Nonviolent Communication (NVC) around the world.

Founded in 1984 by Dr. Marshall B. Rosenberg, CNVC has been contributing to a vast social transformation in thinking, speaking and acting— showing people how to connect in ways that inspire compassionate results. NVC is now being taught around the globe in communities, schools, prisons, mediation centers, churches, businesses, professional conferences, and more. Hundreds of certified trainers and hundreds more supporters teach NVC to tens of thousands of people each year in more than 60 countries.

CNVC believes that NVC training is a crucial step to continue building a compassionate, peaceful society. Your tax-deductible donation will help CNVC continue to provide training in some of the most impoverished, violent corners of the world. It will also support the development and continuation of organized projects aimed at bringing NVC training to high-need geographic regions and populations.

To make a tax-deductible donation or to learn more about the valuable resources described below, visit the CNVC website at www.CNVC.org:

- **Training and Certification**—Find local, national, and international training opportunities, access trainer certification information, connect to local NVC communities, trainers, and more.

- **CNVC Bookstore**—Find mail or phone order information for a complete selection of NVC books, booklets, audio, and video materials at the CNVC website.

- **CNVC Projects**—Participate in one of the several regional and theme-based projects that provide focus and leadership for teaching NVC in a particular application or geographic region.

- **E-Groups and List Servs**—Join one of several moderated, topic-based NVC e-groups and list servs developed to support individual learning and the continued growth of NVC worldwide.

For more information, please contact CNVC at:

9301 Indian School Rd., NE, Suite 204, Albuquerque, NM 87112-2861
Ph: 505-244-4041 • US Only: 800-255-7696 • Fax: 505-247-0414
Email: cnvc@CNVC.org • Website: www.CNVC.org

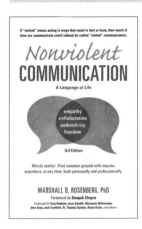

Nonviolent Communication:
A Language of Life, 3rd Edition

Life-Changing Tools for Healthy Relationships

By Marshall B. Rosenberg, PhD

$19.95 — Trade Paper 6x9, 264pp
ISBN: 978-1-892005-28-1

What is Violent Communication?

If "violent" means acting in ways that result in hurt or harm, then much of how we communicate— judging others, bullying, having racial bias, blaming, finger pointing, discriminating, speaking without listening, criticizing others or ourselves, name-calling, reacting when angry, using political rhetoric, being defensive or judging who's "good/bad" or what's "right/wrong" with people—**could indeed be called "violent communication."**

What is Nonviolent Communication?

Nonviolent Communication is the integration of four things:

- **Consciousness:** a set of principles that support living a life of compassion, collaboration, courage, and authenticity

- **Language:** understanding how words contribute to connection or distance

- **Communication:** knowing how to ask for what we want, how to hear others even in disagreement, and how to move toward solutions that work for all

- **Means of influence:** sharing "power with others" rather than using "power over others"

Nonviolent Communication serves our desire to do three things:

- **Increase our ability to live with choice, meaning, and connection**

- **Connect empathically with self and others to have more satisfying relationships**

- **Sharing of resources so everyone is able to benefit**

MORE THAN 1,000 AMAZON REVIEWS—OVER 94% 4-STAR AND 5-STAR!

Available from PuddleDancer Press, the Center for Nonviolent Communication, all major bookstores, and Amazon.com. Distributed by Independent Publisher's Group: 800-888-4741.

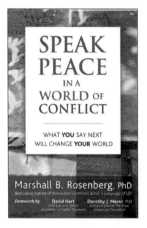

Speak Peace in a World of Conflict

What You Say Next Will Change Your World

By Marshall B. Rosenberg, PhD

$15.95 — Trade Paper 5-3/8x8-3/8, 208pp
ISBN: 978-1-892005-17-5

Create Peace in the Language You Use!

In every interaction, every conversation, and in every thought, you have a choice—to promote peace or perpetuate violence. International peacemaker, mediator, and healer, Dr. Marshall Rosenberg shows you how the language you use is the key to enriching life. Take the first step to reduce violence, heal pain, resolve conflicts, and spread peace on our planet—by developing an internal consciousness of peace rooted in the language you use each day.

Speak Peace is filled with inspiring stories, lessons, and ideas drawn from more than forty years of mediating conflicts and healing relationships in some of the most war-torn, impoverished, and violent corners of the world. *Speak Peace* offers insight, practical skills, and powerful tools that will profoundly change your relationships and the course of your life for the better.

Discover how you can create an internal consciousness of peace as the first step toward effective personal, professional, and social change. Find complete chapters on the mechanics of Speaking Peace, conflict resolution, transforming business culture, transforming enemy images, addressing terrorism, transforming authoritarian structures, expressing and receiving gratitude, and social change.

"Speak Peace **is a book that comes at an appropriate time when anger and violence dominates human attitudes. Marshall Rosenberg gives us the means to create peace through our speech and communication. A brilliant book."**

—**Arun Gandhi**, president, M. K. Gandhi Institute for Nonviolence, USA

"Speak Peace **sums up decades of healing and peacework. It would be hard to list all the kinds of people who can benefit from reading this book, because it's really any and all of us."**

—**Dr. Michael Nagler**, author, America Without Violence and Is There No Other Way: A Search for a Nonviolent Future

Available from PuddleDancer Press, the Center for Nonviolent Communication, all major bookstores, and Amazon.com. Distributed by Independent Publisher's Group: 800-888-4741.

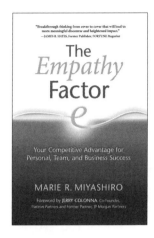

The Empathy Factor

Your Competitive Advantage for Personal, Team, and Business Success

By Marie R. Miyashiro, APR

$19.95 — Trade Paper 6x9, 256pp
ISBN: 978-1-892005-25-0

The Transformative Power of Empathy!

With In this groundbreaking book, award-winning communication and organizational strategist Marie Miyashiro explores the missing element leaders must employ to build profits and productivity in the new economy—Empathy.

Building from the latest research about organizational effectiveness, emotional aptitude in the workplace, and brain science, Miyashiro offers both real-world insight and a practical framework to bring the transformative power of empathy to your entire organization.

Miyashiro's approach combines more than 26 years of experience advising for-profit companies, government agencies, and nonprofits to substantially improve their organizational communication with a proven, world-renowned process from the largest empathy-based community in the world.

The Empathy Factor takes Dr. Marshall Rosenberg's work developing Compassionate Communication into the business community by introducing *Integrated Clarity®*—a powerful framework you can use to understand and effectively meet the critical needs of your organization without compromising those of your employees or customers.

"**Breakthrough thinking from cover to cover.** *The Empathy Factor* **will help thoughtful business people add substance and dimension to relationships within the workforce—colleagues and customers.**"

—JAMES B. HAYES, Former Publisher, FORTUNE Magazine

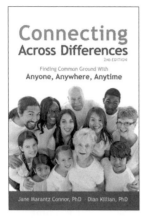

Connecting Across Differences, 2nd Edition

Finding Common Ground With Anyone, Anywhere, Anytime

By Jane Marantz Connor, PhD and Dian Killian, PhD

$19.95 — Trade Paper 6x9, 416pp
ISBN: 978-1-892005-24-3

Profound Connection Is Just a Conversation Away!

In this fully revised second edition, Dr. Dian Killian and Dr. Jane Marantz Connor offer a comprehensive and accessible guide for exploring the concepts, applications, and transformative power of the Nonviolent Communication process. Discover simple, yet transformative skills to create a life of abundance, where building the personal, professional, and community connections you long for begins with a simple shift in thinking.

Now with an expanded selection of broadly applicable exercises, role-plays, and activities that challenge readers to immediately apply the concepts in everyday life, this new edition opens the authors' insight to an even broader audience. Detailed and comprehensive, this combined book and workbook enhances communication skills by introducing the basic NVC model, as well as more advanced NVC practices.

Relevant, meaningful exercises follow each concept, giving readers the chance to immediately apply the skills they've learned to real life experiences.

Drawing on a combined 25 years of experience, the authors help readers to:
- Transform negative self-talk into self empowerment
- Foster trust and collaboration when stakes are high
- Establish healthy relationships to satisfy your needs
- Defuse anger, enemy images, and other barriers to connection
- Get what you want while maintaining respect and integrity

In each chapter, numerous exercises invite readers to apply NVC skills and concepts in their own lives. The second part features extensive dialogues illustrating NVC in action including in self-empathy, empathy, and mediation. The book closes with a resource guide for further learning and an interview with Marshall Rosenberg from the February 2003 *Sun Magazine*.

Available from PuddleDancer Press, the Center for Nonviolent Communication, all major bookstores, and Amazon.com. Distributed by Independent Publisher's Group: 800-888-4741.

About the Author

IKE LASATER, JD, MCP, Author, Mediator, Trainer, and Speaker, helps organizations and individuals increase their conflict navigation skills and the capacity to use those skills in challenging situations. He also acts as a private mediator, facilitating conversations and connection among people in conflict.

A former civil trial attorney, Lasater cofounded a twenty-person law firm, litigating complex, multi-party commercial and environmental cases for twenty years in the state and federal courts of California. He received a master's degree in city planning from the University of California–Berkeley studying global energy policy. Lasater trained extensively with psychologist Marshall B. Rosenberg, PhD, founder of Nonviolent Communication (NVC) for more than a decade, he grew to see that conflict can be an opportunity for connection, and shifted his focus from law to training. NVC's approach was congruent with his values, developed through long-term practices of Zen meditation, yoga (he cofounded *The Yoga Journal* in 1975), and aikido.

Lasater and colleague John Kinyon codeveloped a yearlong immersion training program that is now offered in five countries. (See www.mediate yourlife.com.)

Lasater has served on the boards of directors of the Center for Nonviolent Communication, the Association for Dispute Resolution of Northern California, the California Yoga Teachers Association, The Lawyers Club of San Francisco, the Yale Humanist Community and on the mediation panel for the United States District Court for the Northern District of California.

He has been a guest speaker at Fontys University of Applied Sciences and The HAN University of Applied Sciences in The Netherlands, the University of California–Berkeley, and the Yale School of Management. Lasater has facilitated workshops in more than more than twenty countries in North and South America, Europe, Africa, Australia, and Asia for such groups as the Dongfeng Nissan car manufacturing plant in Guangzhou, China, BNI in South Korea (with participants from Hyundai and Samsung), Decathlon in Italy, Glynwood in Cold Spring, New York, and in Cleveland, Ohio, the Cleveland Metropolitan Bar Association, The Center for Principled Family Advocacy and The Mediation Association of Northeast Ohio. His mediations include large-scale projects with the University of California–Santa Cruz involving one hundred administrative leaders, and a departmental faculty at the University of California–Los Angeles.

In the wake of the 9/11 attacks, in early 2002, Lasater and his Mediate Your Life cofounder John Kinyon traveled to Afghan refugee camps in Pakistan to offer conflict resolution skills training to elder leaders. And with colleagues at Ayeish, in Spring 2016, he worked with Syrian political opposition leaders of the Etilaf National Coalition of Syrian Revolution and Opposition Forces in Istanbul to offer tools for connection and communication in the midst of intense conflict and negotiation.

For more information about Ike and his work, please visit **ikelasater.com**, where you may also sign up for his mailing list.

You will also find Ike on social media:
Facebook: **facebook.com/IkeLasaterPage**
Twitter: **twitter.com/ikelasater**

To access training videos related to many of the exercises practiced in Ike's workshops, please visit
www.mediateyourlife.com/practice-video-series

Workplace Articles by Ike Lasater

- *New York Times:* What Google Learned From Its Quest to Build the Perfect Team
- *Fast Company*: 3 Ways Companies Are Changing The Dreaded Performance Review
- *Harvard Business Review*: "Fixing Performance Appraisal Is About More than Ditching Annual Reviews"
- *The Library Journal:* "Rethinking the Much-Dreaded Employee Evaluation"
- *Harvard Business Review:* "GE's Real Time Performance Development"
- *Quartz:* Why GE had to kill its annual performance reviews after more than three decades
- *Harvard Business Review:* "Reinventing Performance Management"
- *Fortune:* "IBM Is Blowing Up Its Annual Performance Review"
- *Harvard Business Review:* How to Get Senior Leaders to Change
- *Inc.*: Is Your Leadership Showing?
- *Inc.*: Make a Great First Impression: 7 Smart Tricks
- Business Insider: 5 Secrets of Great Bosses
- *Strategic Leadership Studies:* Transformational Leadership
- *Forbes*: Millennials In the Workplace: They Don't Need Trophies But They Want Reinforcement
- *Harvard Business Review:* The Research We've Ignored About Happiness at Work

Books by Ike Lasater

All books are available for purchase on Amazon (Paperback or Kindle).

***Words That Work in Business: A Practical Guide to Effective Communication in the Workplace,* 2nd Edition**
by Ike Lasater with Julie Stiles

Includes 52 New Workplace Communication tips. Addressing the most common workplace relationship challenges, this practical guide shows how to use the principles of Nonviolent Communication to improve the workplace atmosphere. Offering practical tools that match recognizable work scenarios, this guide can help all employees positively affect their work relationships and company culture, regardless of their position. (Also available from nonviolentcommunication.com)

Choosing Peace: New Ways to Communicate to Reduce Stress, Create Connection, and Resolve Conflict
by Ike Lasater and John Kinyon, with Julie Stiles and Mary Sitze

Choosing Peace is about creating inner peace and from that creating peace with others. In it, we give the reader concrete tools with which to do this. It is a practical hands-on book, a relevant and accessible tool for readers no matter their prior familiarity with our work, or Nonviolent Communication.

Book One in the *Mediate Your Life* series, *A Guide to Removing Barriers to Communication.*

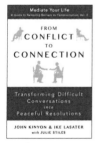

From Conflict to Connection: Transforming Difficult Conversations into Peaceful Resolutions
by Ike Lasater & John Kinyon with Julie Stiles

Everyone experiences conflict, and if you are like most people, it is typically a source of stress or even strife, within relationships. But what if you could have difficult conversations with ease and create agreements that actually work?

With forty years of combined experience in a Nonviolent Communication approach to mediation and conflict resolution, the authors of *From Conflict to Connection* offer a step-by-step guide to being in a relationship with yourself and others that generates new possibilities out of discord and disagreements. If you are ready to escape the power struggle of relationships, be able to hear the other person and express what you would like to say, and find solutions that work for everyone, *From Conflict to Connection* provides a new way forward that has transformed the lives of people worldwide.

Book Two in the *Mediate Your Life* series, *A Guide to Removing Barriers to Communication.*

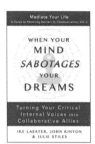

When Your Mind Sabotages Your Dreams: Turning Your Critical Internal Voices Into Collaborative Allies
by Ike Lasater, John Kinyon & Julie Stiles

If you have ever had a dream and then talked yourself out of it, you have experienced internal conflict. The biggest barriers many people face in creating their lives are the self-sabotaging voices that arise within. Learn concrete and practical tools and exercises to mediate internal conflict that will help you stay connected to yourself while you take action to live the life you desire.

Based on the work of *Mediate Your Life*, *When Your Mind Sabotages Your Dreams* is written by authors with nearly 40 years combined experience in a Nonviolent Communication approach to mediation and conflict resolution, who have trained thousands of people worldwide.

Book Three in the *Mediate Your Life* series, *A Guide to Removing Barriers to Communication.*

Mediate Your Life Training Manual, 5th edition
by John Kinyon and Ike Lasater

The *Mediate Your Life* immersion training program supports people in mediating conflict between warring parts of themselves, between self and others, and between others. In three workshops spread over ten months, participants learn to:

• Bring more confidence and ease to dealing with conflict in their lives
• Use the *Mediate Your Life* skills to effectively resolve conflict, heal relationships, and contribute to their own and others' well-being
• Help others who are in conflict

The *Mediate Your Life Training Manual* accompanies the immersion program and includes all of the maps and skills covered in the workshops.

What We Say Matters: Practicing Nonviolent Communication
by Judith Hanson Lasater and Ike Lasater

For yoga teacher Judith Hanson Lasater and mediator Ike K. Lasater, language is a spiritual practice based on giving and receiving with compassion. In *What We Say Matters*, they offer new and nurturing ways of communicating.

Long-term students of yoga and Buddhism, the authors here blend the yoga principle of *satya* (truth) and the Buddhist precept of right speech with Marshall Rosenberg's groundbreaking techniques of Nonviolent Communication (NVC) in a fresh formula for promoting peace at home, at work, and in the world.

The authors offer practical exercises to help readers in any field learn to diffuse anger; make requests rather than demands or assign blame; understand the difference between feelings and needs; recognize how they strategize to get needs met; choose connection over conflict; and extend empathy to themselves and others.